# The Algonquin

## HEATHER KISSOCK

**Weigl**

CALGARY
www.weigl.com

Published by Weigl Educational Publishers Limited
6325 10 Street SE
Calgary, Alberta, Canada
T2H 2Z9

Website: www.weigl.com
Copyright ©2009 Weigl Educational Publishers Limited

Library and Archives Canada Cataloguing in Publication data available upon request.
Fax (403) 233-7769 for the attention of the Publishing Records department.

ISBN 978-1-55388-430-9 (hard cover)
ISBN 978-1-55388-431-6 (soft cover)

Printed in the United States of America
1 2 3 4 5 6 7 8 9 0  12 11 10 09 08

**Project Coordinator** Heather Kissock  **Design** Janine Vangool  **Layout** Terry Paulhus
**Validator** Sheila Staats, GoodMinds.com

**Photograph credits**
Every reasonable effort has been made to trace ownership and to obtain permission to reprint copyright
material. The publishers would be pleased to have any errors or omissions brought to their attention so
that they may be corrected in subsequent printings.

Cover: McCord Museum (main), Newscom (top left), Getty Images (top centre), Newscom (top right) ; Alamy: pages
5, 6, 8, 12, 26T, 28, 29; Canadian Museum of Civilization: pages 3 (III-X-270, D2004-28126), 11T (III-L-182, D2003-15361),
11B (III-X-270, D2004-28126), 14T (III-L-139, D2003-15199), 14M (III-L-193, D2003-15229), 14B (III-L-290, D2003-15315), 15T
(III-L-380 a-b), 20 (III-L-416 a,c, D2003-15390), 24 (III-L-301 a,b, D2003-15121), 25L (III-L-479, D2003-15367), 26B (III-L-150
a,b, D2003-17985), 30 (III-L-124, D2003-15362); Corbis: page 7; CP Images: pages 1, 9, 17, 21, 22; Getty Images: pages 13,
16, 18, 23; McCord Museum: page 10; Nadia Myre/SODART: page 27; Newscom: pages 19, 25R; With permission of the
Royal Ontario Museum © ROM: page 15B.

We acknowledge the financial support of the Government of Canada through the Book Publishing Industry
Development Program (BPIDP) for our publishing activities.

**Please note**
All of the Internet URLs given in the book were valid at the time of publication. However, due to the dynamic
nature of the Internet, some addresses may have changed, or sites may have ceased to exist since publication.
While the author and publisher regret any inconvenience this may cause readers, no responsibility for any such
changes can be accepted by either the author or the publisher.

# CONTENTS

# The People

The Algonquin are a **First Nation** that live in the Ottawa Valley, along the border between Ontario and Quebec. Algonquin **oral** history shows that the Algonquin moved to the area from the Atlantic coast at least 600 years ago. Here, they went from site to site following the **migration** routes of the animals they hunted. By the time European explorers arrived in the area, the Algonquin knew the land well and helped greatly in the development of the fur trade.

## Algonquin Map

This map shows the traditional lands of the Algonquin in Canada.

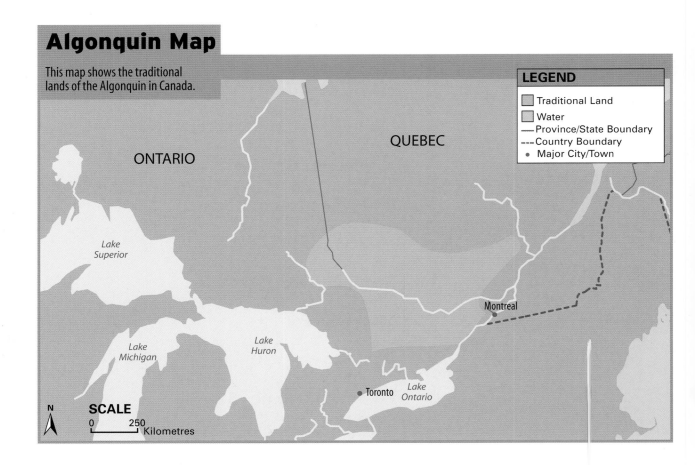

**LEGEND**
- ☐ Traditional Land
- ☐ Water
- — Province/State Boundary
- --- Country Boundary
- • Major City/Town

ONTARIO

QUEBEC

Lake Superior

Lake Michigan

Lake Huron

Montreal

Toronto

Lake Ontario

N

**SCALE**

0    250 Kilometres

French explorers first met the Algonquin in the Ottawa Valley in 1603. The French formed a fur-trading relationship with the Algonquin. When the British arrived in the area, they became allies with the Iroquois, who were enemies of the Algonquin. The Iroquois and the Algonquin battled for trading routes for the next 100 years. When the fur trade era drew to an end, the two groups began to work together to deal with European settlement of their traditional lands.

Today, there are about 8,000 Algonquin living in Canada. Some live in cities and towns, but most live on one of 10 **reserves**. Nine of these reserves are located in Quebec, with the remaining one found in Ontario.

The Algonquin call themselves the *Anishnabe*, or "original person." This word is very similar to the word they use to describe all **Aboriginal Peoples**, so they use Algonquin to identify themselves within the Aboriginal community. The word *Algonquin* has an uncertain origin. Some people believe it comes from the Maliseet word *elehgumoqik*, which means "**allies**." Others believe it comes from *Algoomaking*, a Mi'kmaq place name. Both Algonquin and Algonkin are accepted spellings.

**The Ottawa Valley is known for its rolling woodlands and fresh waters.**

# Algonquin Homes

The **traditional** home of the Algonquin was the wigwam. These dome-shaped structures were easy to put together as they were made from local materials. They were sturdy and able to withstand all sorts of conditions. These features suited the active lifestyle of the Algonquin. The Algonquin could easily move their homes to follow animals as needed.

A wigwam was made using trees and bark. To make the frame, the Algonquin would find young trees called saplings that were 3 to 4.5 metres long. Saplings were flexible and could be bent into the curved shape of the wigwam. The saplings were placed over a circle pattern that had been drawn in the ground. The tallest saplings arched over the centre of the circle, while smaller trees were placed on the outside. Another set of saplings was wrapped around the arches to provide support. All the saplings were tied together. The wigwam was complete when layers of bark were placed over the frame.

Wigwams ranged in size. Some were meant for only one person. Others could house up to four families.

When the Algonquin moved, they would often take the wigwam's covering with them, but leave the poles behind. This way, they would not have to rebuild the frame when they returned to the area.

# DWELLING AND DECORATION

Wigwams provided shelter from the weather. However, they also contained many items the Algonquin needed to survive.

In the centre of each wigwam was a firepit, which the Algonquin used for warmth and cooking. The smoke from the fire escaped through a hole in the top of the wigwam. Life inside the wigwam revolved around the fire. Reed mats placed around the pit were used for sleeping and relaxing. The Algonquin covered themselves with hides and furs to help keep warm.

Cooking was done over the firepit in the centre of the wigwam.

Baskets and shelf-like structures were found throughout the wigwam. The baskets often held corn, berries, and other food items. Pots and dishes sat on or were hung from the shelves. In some homes, a large cooking pot was hung from a hook in the roof of the wigwam. In others, the pot was hung from poles that had been pounded into the ground. Most household items were made from wood, but metal became common after contact with Europeans.

# Algonquin Communities

Traditional Algonquin society was patriarchal. This means that leadership and power was passed along the male side of the family. Fathers handed their hunting grounds down to their sons. When couples married, they lived with the husband's family. Even the role of chief stayed within one family, normally going from father to oldest son.

The chief in an Algonquin community was called an *ogima*. He acted as the spokesperson for the group but did not have sole authority over the people. Decision-making was a cooperative process that involved all members of the community. The men and women of the community would meet to discuss a problem or situation and would come to a solution or decision as a group.

When European fur traders arrived in the area, the Algonquin started building their villages near trading posts.

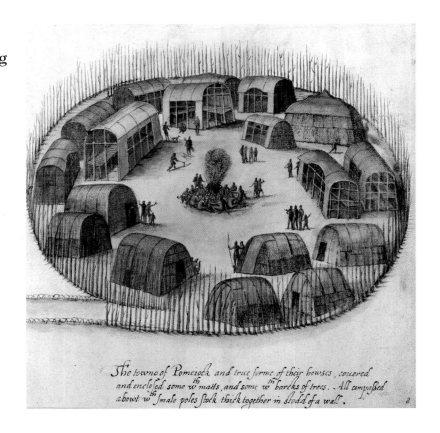

The towne of Pomeiock and true forme of their howses, couered and enclofed some w^th matts, and some w^th barcks of trees. All compaffed abowt w^th fmale poles ftock thick together in ftedd of a wall.

The size of an Algonquin community often depended on the time of year. In the summer months, food was plentiful and easy to find. The Algonquin would come together to fish and socialize. When winter arrived, the group would separate into smaller family units for hunting.

No matter what size the group was, everyone had a role to play. Men were responsible for hunting and protecting the group from enemies. Women gathered berries and other food. They also cooked, made clothes, and cared for children. When they were old enough, children were expected to help the adults with their work.

The Algonquin no longer move from place to place with the seasons. Instead, most Algonquin live on reserves in permanent housing and have full-time jobs. Algonquin children attend school. They learn about Algonquin traditions from family and community members.

The patriarchal leadership of the past is also gone. Today, chiefs are elected by the community through a majority vote. Both men and women can become chief. The chief is supported by a council that assists in making decisions regarding the reserve and its citizens.

**Today, the Algonquin have their own police force to help keep order.**

# Algonquin Clothing

Following animal herds was necessary to the Algonquin's survival in the past. The animals served as food sources. They also provided the Algonquin with the clothes they wore. Furs, hides, and feathers were all put to use in making clothing for the Algonquin. Moose, deer, beaver, muskrat, bear, and even partridges were just some of the animals that supplied materials for Algonquin clothing.

The arrival of Europeans influenced Algonquin clothing. The Algonquin began to make clothing that looked like that of the newcomers.

The Algonquin needed clothing for a range of weather. During the warm months of summer, men wore loincloths, or pieces of moose or deer hide that covered the lower parts of their body. Women wore sleeveless, **tunic**-style dresses, also made from hides.

An Algonquin mother carried her baby on her back using a cradleboard.

In the winter months, women would sew sleeves onto their dresses to better protect themselves from the cold. Both men and women wore moose or deerskin leggings. Bear furs were used as capes, while the furs of muskrats and beavers were made into mittens and toques. The Algonquin wore **moccasins** made from animal hides throughout the year.

Algonquin children were dressed in clothing similar to adults. However, newborns were sometimes dressed in pure white deerskins. It was a traditional belief that the colour white would chase evil spirits away and keep the children safe.

Headgear was another part of Algonquin clothing. Some headdresses were worn for ceremonies or decoration. The men often wore a headdress called a hair roach. This was a strip of porcupine hair that sat on the back of the head. Roaches sometimes had feathers attached as decoration. Chiefs were known to wear more elaborate headdresses.

While the men were known as the hunters, women sometimes hunted as well. One of the animals they tracked was the partridge. To disguise themselves from the bird, the women would wear a headdress that featured partridge tail feathers. The feathers were attached to a headband made of tree bark. Some women wore partridge wings in their hair when hunting instead.

Headdresses could be made entirely of feathers or have feathers as decoration.

# Algonquin Food

The Algonquin were known as hunter-gatherers. This means that they mainly relied on food provided by nature. These foods included many plants and animals.

Deer and moose were staple meats for the Algonquin. However, smaller animals, such as rabbits and birds, were hunted as well. The meat was eaten on its own or put in soups and stews. To store it for winter use, meat was often combined with berries and dried to make *pimikan*. This dried meat provided the Algonquin with food when animals were difficult to locate.

**Snowberries were boiled with mint to make tea.**

In the summer months, the women spent much of their time searching for plants and preparing food with what they found. The Algonquin had a varied diet. Salads were made by mixing watercress, wood sorel, wild onions, and dandelions. Maple syrup and sunflower oil were mixed to make the salad's dressing. The Algonquin made a variety of soups as well. One soup, *paganens*, was made using hazelnuts.

## Paganens (Wild Nut Soup)

Ingredients

710 millilitres of hazelnuts, crushed

6 shallots, with tops

45 mL of parsley, chopped

1.5 litres of soup stock

5 mL salt

1.2 mL teaspoon black pepper

Equipment

**Cooking pot**

**Spoon**

Directions

1. Place all of the ingredients in a large pot.

2. Cook at medium heat until the mixture reaches a simmer.

3. Let the soup simmer for 1.5 hours. Stir occasionally.

# Algonquin Tools

Nature provided the Algonquin with the resources they needed to make their traditional tools. Animals supplied bones, leather, **sinew**, and antlers. Other tools were made using rocks and the wood and bark of trees. Due to their active lifestyle, the Algonquin preferred not to carry many items with them as they moved from camp to camp. They would leave tools behind when they moved, making new ones as they were needed.

Many Algonquin tools were used in hunting. Traps and snares were used to catch an animal. A trap often was made from a log that dropped down on an animal when it took **bait** placed below the log. Snares made of strips of leather or sinew looped around the animal when it tried to take the bait. Once the animal was captured, the Algonquin used bows and arrows, axes, spears, and knives to prepare it for camp. All of these tools were made of sharpened stones that were tied to pieces of wood or bone with sinew.

At camp, the women had tools that helped them with their work. Birchbark was used to make food containers. Animal bones were carved to make needles and **awls**. Both were used to sew clothing. When stitching items together, sinew served as thread.

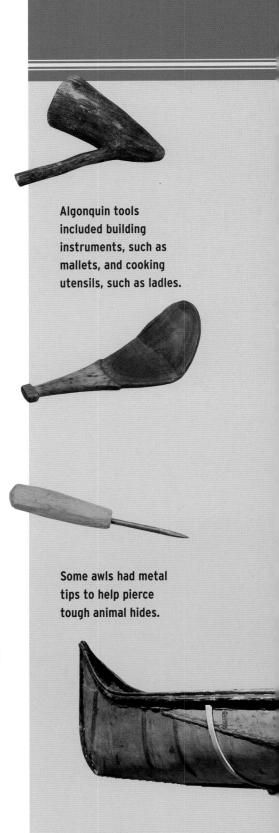

Algonquin tools included building instruments, such as mallets, and cooking utensils, such as ladles.

Some awls had metal tips to help pierce tough animal hides.

# TRANSPORTATION

The Algonquin needed special tools to help them easily move from place to place. They used equipment that were geared to the weather and the distance to be travelled.

In the summer months, travelling short distances was done by foot. This was helpful when hunting because it allowed the Algonquin to quietly approach prey. However, the summer months were also the best time to meet and trade with other Aboriginal groups and Europeans. This required the Algonquin to travel longer distances. As water travel allowed for a faster trip than foot travel, the Algonquin relied on canoes for this type of journey. Algonquin canoes were normally made of birchbark and had upturned ends that allowed the boat to slice sharply through the water.

The waters were frozen over the winter months, so canoes were not an option for travel. Most winter travel was done by foot. The Algonquin used snowshoes to keep them from sinking or getting stuck in the snow. The paddle-like shape of the frame and the **latticed** strips of leather helped the Algonquin stay on top of the snow and move more quickly.

Some Algonquin wore bearpaw snowshoes. These snowshoes were tailless, allowing the wearer to move through woods and hilly areas with ease.

The bark cover of an Algonquin canoe was often lined with thin pieces of wood.

# Algonquin Religion

Algonquin religion was based on the natural world. The Algonquin believed in a life force, called *Manitou*, that existed in all things. People, animals, rocks, and trees all had this life force within them. Watching over the Algonquin and their world was their creator or Great Spirit, *Kitchi Manitou*. This spirit was neither male nor female and did not exist in human form.

To the Algonquin, Kitchi Manitou was the Sun that shone down from the sky, playing a role in the life of everything on Earth.

Other spirits lived among the Algonquin as well, offering them guidance and protection. Within Algonquin communities were **shamans**, who were believed to have special relationships with the spirits. These shamans could be called upon when the people needed spiritual help. They worked hard to maintain a healthy community.

The Algonquin believed that *Djasakids* were shamans that could consult the spirits about the future. They would seek guidance and support for problems facing the community. *Wabenos* focused their attention on hunting. These shamans would use medicines and powders to ensure men had a successful hunt. The *Midewiwin* were responsible for keeping traditional Algonquin customs and beliefs alive. They were healers, who used medicines to help people who were ill.

The Algonquin believed that everyone had a relationship with the spirits, including Kitchi Manitou. They could communicate with the spirits at any time for any reason. Often, this communication took the form of prayer. Sometimes, a person would embark on a vision quest, especially if he or she was facing a problem.

During a vision quest, the person would leave the community to spend time alone in nature. This time could be spent in many ways, including drumming, fasting, or praying. This was done until a spirit, usually in the form of an animal, appeared. The spirit would help the person by providing advice or by agreeing to become the person's **guardian**.

**Peace pipes are used by Algonquin spiritual leaders for certain ceremonies.**

# Ceremonies and Celebrations

Many Algonquin ceremonies and celebrations are based on the group's spirituality. Some of these ceremonies are performed only by shamans. Others can be performed by individuals. Still others are performed by a group of people. Each ceremony has its own purpose and meaning to the Algonquin.

Djasakids are known for their tent shaking ceremonies. In this ceremony, the shaman entered a tent or wigwam that had been specially made for the ritual. The shaman would spend an entire night singing and playing the drum in order to call the spirits to the tent. If the spirits did appear, the tent would start to shake, and the sounds of animal calls would be heard coming from within the tent. The animal spirits would give the Djasakid advice and direction about a specific problem.

The Algonquin believed that animal spirits could provide them with guidance and solutions to problems.

When performing the smudge ceremony, the Algonquin made sure to fan the smoke into their hair. The Algonquin believed that hair collected the energy around them.

Sometimes, people felt the need to cleanse themselves or to rid themselves of negative influences. The smudge ceremony helped them do this. During this ceremony, the person would burn plants and herbs and then fan the smoke toward him or her. In doing this, the spirit within the plant would reach the person and provide the cleansing that was needed. Two of the most common plants used in smudge ceremonies were sage and sweetgrass. Sage was believed to remove negative energy, and sweetgrass was thought to bring positive energy.

One of the best-known First Nations celebrations is the powwow. The word "powwow" comes from the Algonquin word *pauwau*, or "gathering." Originally, the powwow was a time when spiritual leaders held a meeting. Over the years, it became a time for different Algonquin groups to get together and renew relationships. They did this by singing, dancing, drumming, and feasting. Today, powwows are a time of celebration that people of all nations are welcome to attend.

# WEDDINGS

Algonquin weddings were big celebrations. They were usually held in the summer when many Algonquin gathered as one large group.

Before a couple married, they chose four people to be their sponsors. As sponsors, it was their job to help the couple have a successful marriage.

The ceremony was performed by a man called the pipe carrier. It was his job to make sure that the couple was serious about their relationship. The pipe carrier did not perform the ceremony unless he was sure that the couple was committed to being married.

At the ceremony, the couple expressed their intent to become husband and wife, and the sponsors promised to support them. The couple shared the pipe that the pipe carrier offered them. Then, they presented him with a gift.

Following the ceremony, people feasted, sang, and danced. At the end of the night, the couple gave each guest a small gift.

# Music and Dance

Music was an important part of life in Algonquin society. Singing and playing instruments took place on a daily basis and for a variety of reasons. Due to the importance of song in the community, the Algonquin found many ways to express themselves musically.

The drum played a key role in Algonquin music. To the Algonquin, the beating of a drum represented the beating of a heart, the source of life. Drumming was held in such high regard that the Algonquin developed several kinds of drums. The grandfather drum was made from a hollow log covered with an animal skin. The grandmother drum consisted of birchbark covered with beaver skin. The man's drum was made from cedar, with moose sinew as its covering. This drum could be played on both ends. The girl, or rain, drum was filled with water to create a unique sound.

Rattles, flutes, and whistles were other instruments the Algonquin used to make music. Moose hoofs, turtle claws, and hoops of cedar could all be used to create rattles. Flutes and whistles were carved from hazelwood. The Algonquin are thought to have developed a violin-like instrument. Its body was made from wood, and moose sinew became its strings.

Each of the four drums symbolized a direction. The grandfather drum represented north, the grandmother drum was south, the man's drum was west, and the rain drum stood for the west.

# SINGING AND DANCING

Most Algonquin songs were related to natural events in daily life. The rise and fall of the Sun, flying geese, and hunting all had songs created about them. Some of these songs were accompanied by dancing.

The appearance of the Sun in the sky was a reason to sing and give thanks. The Algonquin often began their day paying tribute to the Sun in this way. At the end of the day, they honoured and gave thanks to the Sun again. As it began to set, the Algonquin would form a circle and begin to dance, singing as they moved.

Hunting stories often were told through a combination of song and dance. One song was a call to deer. While singing it, the Algonquin would create a dance by copying the movements of deer. Another song told how bird calls directed hunters to nearby deer.

A song was made for migrating geese. The sounds created by the singers' voices were similar to the sounds of wings beating.

Today, performing traditional dances is seen as a way to educate others about Algonquin traditions and customs.

# Language and Storytelling

The Algonquin language belongs to the Algonquian language family. This is a group of languages that share common features. Considered the most widespread First Nations language family in North America, it also includes the languages of several other groups, including the Cree, Ojibwa, and Blackfoot.

Unlike many other First Nations languages, Algonquin is in no danger of disappearing. More than 60 percent of the Algonquin in Quebec speak Algonquin as their first language. Algonquin living in Ontario also speak their traditional language, but younger generations speak French or English more often. Algonquin is taught in the Algonquin school system from daycare to grade 12.

The Algonquin community is doing much to ensure that younger generations learn their traditional language.

One way the language is taught is through traditional stories. Storytellers visit daycares and school classrooms to pass along stories that are generations old. In doing this, the Algonquin language is maintained, and the **core values** of the Algonquin are passed on. Many Algonquin stories offer their listeners lessons about life and human behaviour. They feature characters well known to the Algonquin, including Nanabozho, Nokomis, and Widjigo. Nanabozho is a heroic figure who plays a major role in Algonquin **creation stories**. Nokomis is a grandmother figure who often uses her wisdom to help others. Widjigo is an evil spirit. People who have committed evil deeds are sometimes turned into Widjigos as punishment.

**The muskrat holds a special place in Algonquin folklore.**

# NANABOZHO'S FLOOD

Nanabozho was relaxing along the bank of a river, when he noticed the water beginning to rise. He moved farther back on the land, trying to keep out of the rising waters. He finally found himself on the top of a mountain. With the water continuing to rise, Nanabozho knew that he had to find somewhere else to go and a way to get there. He quickly grabbed two logs and made a raft.

As he rode the water's current, he saw many of his animal friends panicking that they might drown in the flood. He called to them, asking them to try to find him some soil. Only the muskrat responded, bringing him a small handful of soil. Nanabozho looked down at the soil and gently blew on it. The soil spread out and grew, creating the land on which we now live.

# Algonquin Art

Nature played an important role in Algonquin art. The Algonquin used items found in nature to create their art, and they expressed their respect for the natural world in their works. Floral **motifs** were one of the most common designs found in Algonquin art. The patterns were etched onto baskets or beaded onto clothing items.

The Algonquin used natural materials to make baskets. The most common materials were sweetgrass, ash, and birchbark. Sweetgrass baskets were made by forming coils from the grass and then spiraling the coils into the basket's shape. Ash baskets were a woven form of basket. The men would cut down the tree and prepare the strips of bark needed for weaving. The women would then weave the strips into a basket. To make a birchbark basket, the bark was moistened and moulded into shape. The pieces were bound together with animal sinew. Birchbark baskets were decorated with porcupine quills. Sometimes, they had patterns **etched** onto them.

The Algonquin created many items using birchbark, from baskets to canoes.

Etching can be found on many traditional Algonquin birchbark items, from baskets to moose callers to canoes. The etching was done on the dark inner side of the bark, which was usually placed on the outside of the object. To etch the pattern onto the bark, the dark layers would be scraped away to make a pattern in the lighter layers underneath.

To put patterns on clothing items, the Algonquin used quills and beads. Before European contact, beads were made from small pieces of shells. Quills or shell pieces were sewn onto clothing in flower petal shapes. When the Europeans arrived, they introduced multi-coloured glass beads. The Algonquin used the beads to create more detailed flower designs.

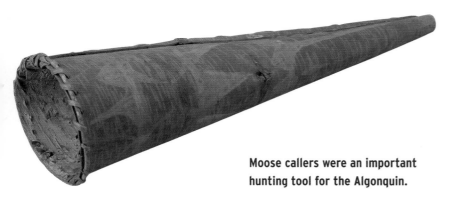

Moose callers were an important hunting tool for the Algonquin.

The making of **wampum** combined Algonquin artistry with their communication skills. Wampum belts were made using white and purple shell beads. The purple often served as the background colour, while the white beads were sewn into patterns. These patterns could explain the wearer's family history or commemorate an event. At first, the belts were used as a communication tool. When a messenger was sent to another community, he often took a wampum belt with him to explain the purpose of his journey to the other people. **Elders** used wampum belts as historical records. When Europeans arrived, wampum belts became a form of money. They were traded for items the Algonquin needed.

# Body Painting

Besides decorating baskets and clothing, the Algonquin also decorated themselves with the use of dyes. Most often, body painting was done for special occasions, such as ceremonies and feasts.

The dyes came in a variety of colours, ranging from yellow to red to black. All of them came directly from nature. Plants, clay, and ashes could all be used to make the dyes.

**Bloodroot plants provided the Algonquin with red dye.**

Everyone had unique markings that were applied to their face and body. Women would find and mix the dyes, and then paint the designs on the people needing them. Some markings were so complex that it would take an entire day to complete one person.

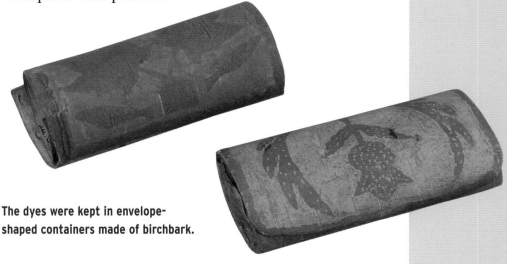

**The dyes were kept in envelope-shaped containers made of birchbark.**

## Nadia Myre

Nadia Myre is a **multi-disciplinary** artist of Algonquin descent. She was born in Montreal, Quebec, in 1974. Following high school, Nadia began to develop her artistic skills. Moving to Vancouver, she attended the Emily Carr Institute of Art and Design. She graduated with a Bachelor of Fine Arts. She followed this with a Master of Fine Arts degree in sculpture from Montreal's Concordia University. Her works are now displayed in galleries throughout Canada and around the world.

Nadia's art reflects the relationship she has had with her First Nations **heritage**. Her mother was born a member of the Kitigan Zibi Anishinabeg band that lived on a reserve in Maniwaki, Quebec. However, she

**Circles play a big part in Algonquin belief systems. To the Algonquin, everything is circular, from the cycle of the seasons to the circle of life.**

lost her band status when she was adopted by a family that did not live on the reserve. This meant that, when Nadia was born, she, too, was not considered to be a member of the band.

In 1985, the Canadian government passed Bill C-31. This bill awarded band status to First Nations people who had lost it through no fault of their own. Nadia was given band status and is now a member of the Kitigan Zibi Anishinabeg band.

These events had a huge impact on Nadia's life and her art. This is shown in her work,

Grandmother's Circle. The central objects of the work are fish-drying racks, a reference to her family's past. A circle around the racks shows the bond of family. On the outside of the circle, Nadia has placed four wooden poles. The poles represent the artist as an outsider in her own family and community.

Nadia has been given many awards and **grants**. She has sat on committees that award grants to other artists. Nadia currently lives in Montreal.

# Studying the Past

Archaeologists locate and study objects from the past, including those of the Algonquin. By examining these **artifacts** and talking with Algonquin elders, archaeologists can develop theories about Algonquin ancestors.

One type of artifact the archaeologists have studied is the **pictograph**. Found throughout Algonquin traditional lands, Algonquin peoples of the past used these rock paintings to communicate with each other. Archaeologists have studied the pictographs and held discussions with the elders about them. Elders have been able to explain what the pictographs mean and why they have been placed where they are. Understanding these paintings is key to learning how the Algonquin lived and what they believed.

Many of these paintings are becoming damaged due to weathering. To make sure that they are not lost, archaeologists are finding ways to preserve and record pictographs. Computer technology is being used to recreate pictographs that are fading. Photographs are taken and then scanned for computer use. By working with the images, details that were almost faded from view can be seen once again. This allows them to be studied in more depth.

Many Algonquin pictographs relate to animal migration cycles and Algonquin spirituality.

# TIMELINE

## About AD 1400
The Algonquin migrate to the Ottawa Valley from the east coast of what is now Canada.

## 1570
The Algonquin and the Iroquois are at war.

## 1603
European explorer Samuel de Champlain meets the Algonquin and begin trading with them.

## 1609-1610
The French support the Algonquin in their war with the Iroquois.

## 1629-1632
France and Great Britain are at war. As Great Britain's allies, the Iroquois gain back much of the land they lost in their war with the Algonquin.

## 1630-1642
Many Algonquin leave the Ottawa Valley and move farther into present-day Quebec.

## 1650
The Iroquois drive out the Algonquin that remained in the Ottawa Valley.

## 1667
The war with the Iroquois comes to an end. Some Algonquin begin to return to the Ottawa Valley.

## 1760
The British gain control of the area. The Algonquin sign a treaty with them, agreeing to remain **neutral** in any future wars the British may have with the French.

## 1983-present
The Algonquin begin the process of reclaiming their traditional lands from the Canadian government.

Samuel de Champlain helped the Algonquin battle the Iroquois in the 1600s.

# Make a Moose Caller

When hunting moose, the Algonquin would use a moose caller to attract the animal to them. Some of these moose callers were simple cones of birchbark. Others were etched with unique designs.

| Materials | | |
|---|---|---|
| | · Bristleboard | · Tape |
| | · Ruler | · Watercolour paint |
| | · Scissors | · Paintbrush |

## Steps

1. Cut the bristleboard into a square about 30.5 centimetres in diameter.

2. Roll the square from one corner to another, making a cone with one end narrow and one end wide.

3. Once the square forms a cone, tape the seam together to hold it in shape. Fold the pieces at the wide end into the cone, and tape them so that the wide end is even all the way around.

4. Paint the outside of the moose caller with a design of your choosing.

5. When the paint dries, try blowing into the cone to see if you can make a sound.

# Further Reading

Find out more about the role of nature in traditional Algonquin life by reading Robert E. Nichols' *Birds of Algonquin Legend* (Regional Publishing Company, 1996).

*Birchbark Canoe: Living Among the Algonquins* (Firefly Books, 1997) recounts the story of how David Gidmark learned about the ways of the Algonquin people while being taught to build an Algonquin canoe.

# Websites

Learn more about the history of the Algonquin people at
www.tolatsga.org/alg.html

See how the Algonquin language compares to Canada's national languages by visiting
www.native-
languages.org/algonquin_words.htm

The stories behind Algonquin music and dance can be explored at
http://nativedance.ca/index.php/Algonquin/Who_We_Are

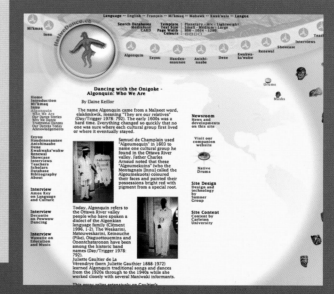

# GLOSSARY

**Aboriginal Peoples:** original inhabitants of a country. In Canada, the term refers to First Nations, Inuit, and Métis

**allies:** friends or supporters

**archaeologists:** people who study ancient societies and the objects they left behind

**artifacts:** items, such as tools, made by humans

**awls:** pointed tools that are used to pierce leather

**bait:** a piece of food used to attract animals to a trap

**core values:** the central beliefs and standards of a person or group

**creation stories:** legends that tell how a group of people came to be on Earth

**elders:** the older and more influential people of a group or community

**etched:** cut a design into an object

**First Nation:** a member of Canada's Aboriginal community who are not Inuit of Métis

**grants:** funding given to artists to help them create art

**guardian:** a person or spirit that watches over and protects someone else

**heritage:** parts of the past that have been handed down to present-day generations

**latticed:** a criss-crossed pattern

**migration:** the movement from one place to another by one large group

**moccasins:** leather footwear worn by many Aboriginal groups

**motifs:** themes that occur throughout a design

**multi-disciplinary:** the use of many art forms

**neutral:** taking no side in an argument

**oral:** spoken, not written

**pictograph:** an image painted on a rock

**reserves:** land the Canadian government set aside for First Nations groups

**shamans:** religious leaders; sometimes called medicine men or women

**sinew:** animal tendon

**traditional:** based on established practices or beliefs

**tunic:** a loose-fitting shirt

**wampum:** beads made from polished shells that had spiritual significance with many First Nations

# INDEX